CITY CYCLING
SAN FRANCISCO

Text by Kelton Wright
Illustrations by Chris McNally

Rapha.

❧ **Thames & Hudson**

Original concept created by
Andrew Edwards and Max Leonard

Thanks to my husband Ben Foster,
and to Susana Muñoz

City Cycling San Francisco © 2018 Thames & Hudson Ltd, London

Designed by Michael Lenz, Draught Associates

Illustrations by Chris McNally

First published in 2017 in the United States of America by
Thames & Hudson Inc., 500 Fifth Avenue, New York, New York 10110

www.thamesandhudsonusa.com

Library of Congress Control Number 2017942159

ISBN 978-0-500-29311-9

Printed and bound in China by Everbest Printing Co. Ltd

CONTENTS

HOW TO USE THIS GUIDE

This San Francisco volume of the *City Cycling* series is designed to give you the confidence to explore the city by bike at your own pace. On the front flaps is a locator map of the whole city to help you orient yourself. Here, you will see five neighbourhoods to explore: Mission (p. 10); Dogpatch and the Embarcadero (p. 16); Downtown and Hayes Valley (p. 22); Castro and Haight-Ashbury (p. 28); and Sunset and Golden Gate Park (p. 34).

Each of these neighbourhoods is easily accessible by bike, and is full of cafés, bars, galleries, museums, shops and parks. All are mapped in detail, and our recommendations for places of interest and where to fuel up on coffee and cake, as well as where to find a WiFi connection, are marked. Take a pootle round on your bike and see what suits you.

If you fancy a set itinerary, turn to A Day On The Bike on the front flaps. It takes you on a relaxed 58-km (36-mile) route through some of the parts of San Francisco we haven't featured in the neighbourhood sections, and visits some of the more touristy sights. Pick and choose the bits you fancy, go from back to front, and use the route as you wish.

A section on Racing and Training (p. 40) fills you in on some of San Francisco's cycling heritage and provides ideas for longer rides if you want to explore the beautiful countryside around the city, while Essential Bike Info (p. 44) discusses road etiquette and the ins and outs of using the cycle-hire scheme and public transportation. Finally, Links and Addresses (p. 48) will give you the practical details you need to know.

SAN FRANCISCO: THE CYCLING CITY

On a map, San Francisco looks like the ideal cycling city, and its compact size of 11 km by 11 km (7 miles by 7 miles) positively begs to be ridden across. It also begs to be ridden up, however – many of the streets here reach grades of over 20 per cent, with some even higher than 30 per cent. These grades are what make San Francisco a city of remarkable vistas. From its high vantage points, you can look out over the water, taking in the famous bridges, or just watch the fog roll in.

In addition to being a city of incredible views and steep hills, San Francisco is also a city of neighbourhoods. The more the population grows, the more of them seem to pop up. Since the California Gold Rush began in 1848, people have been coming here to forge new paths for themselves, whether via its forward-thinking, bohemian cultures or the latest tech boom. The historical influence of each neighbourhood can be seen and felt through the street art, the food, the shops and, of course, the people. From Latin influences in the Mission to buoyant gay pride in the Castro, everyone in San Francisco has a neighbourhood that feels like home and feels distinct.

Thanks to the abundance of opportunity and the open-mindedness of its citizens, San Francisco is now the second most densely populated city in the United States. This density has led to an effort from the city to make it easier for locals and tourists alike to forgo their cars for public transit, walking and, best of all, bikes, with over 300 km, or roughly 200 miles, of bike paths and designated routes. Much of the city is bike-friendly, thanks to the help of the San Francisco Bicycle Coalition (see p. 45). The SFBC was founded in 1971, and by 2011 had over 12,000 members helping to campaign for improved infrastructure, broader access and greater education around bicycles. Whenever better and safer routes pop up around the city, the SFBC likely has had something to do with it.

Two of the best routes for visitors to see the city by bike are the Wiggle and the Embarcadero. The Wiggle, less an actual thing and more of a useful suggestion, is a mile-long, zig-zagging bicycle route that will take you from Market St to Golden Gate Park without ever going above a 6 per cent grade. The route is typically used when going uphill in efforts to avoid the steep stuff, but is applicable downhill, as well – just look for the signs. On the eastern perimeter of the city, you'll find the Embarcadero. The SFBC is hard at work to create protected bikeways here, too, but for now, the green bike lanes do just fine. Ride along it with regular bike commuters to see sweeping views of the Bay Bridge, AT&T Park and the Ferry Building, eventually connecting with North Beach, Fisherman's Wharf and the Marina (more on that in A Day On The Bike).

But no matter what route you take through or around the city, the most quintessential route for visitors is the one that takes you out of it: the Golden Gate Bridge. One of the most beautiful areas of San Francisco comprises Golden Gate Park, the Presidio and the path over the bridge. It can be a cold and blustery ride, but it's worth it just for the view looking back across the bay.

Whether you're visiting for the culture or the views or both, there's no bad time to visit San Francisco. You can find it wrapped in a wet fog, all to yourself in the winter, or sunny and vibrant in early fall. The temperature rarely falls below freezing, but it never gets hot either, with the highs often lingering somewhere between 10 and 20° C (50 and 70° F) all year round. But the city is known for its microclimates, and the key to dressing like a local is layers. In the span of 10 minutes or one block, it can go from pleasant and sunny to cold and foggy. No matter where you're riding, pack a jacket, and enjoy one of the most eclectic, evolving and bike-friendly cities in the United States.

NEIGHBOURHOODS

MISSION

BREAD, COFFEE AND BURRITOS

The Mission District wears its culture on its sleeve. Just riding along Valencia and Mission, the main arteries of the area, will tell you pretty much everything you need to know. Street to street, you'll encounter the aromatic roasting of coffee beans wafting from high-end cafés filled with the new tech elite, see Spanish-language signs directing you to the *bodegas* and *taquerias*, and be dazzled by the array of fancy shops, sidewalk sales, street food, upscale restaurants and some of the best street art in the city. The Mission's spirit is still defined by its Latino community, but the influence of Silicon Valley can be felt here as rents skyrocket and long-time residents are forced to relocate. Expect to do a fair amount of bobbing and weaving through the neighbourhood to take it all in.

To start off on the right foot, stop in at one of the many *panaderias*. **La Mexicana ❶** and **Pan Lido Salvadoreno ❷** are both good places to head to for *pan dulce*. If you're after something with sprinkles, a stop by **Dynamo Donut and Coffee ❸** should satisfy the craving. And if sugar isn't your poison, make your first stop **Craftsman and Wolves ❹** for a delight called 'The Rebel Within', a muffin peppered with green onion and sausage with a soft-boiled egg inside. Whatever your breakfast, coffee is easy to find in the Mission. For the ultimate drip-coffee experience, head to the original location of **Philz Coffee ❺**. And if you've already been to any of the Philz branches, then stop by **Linea Caffe ❻** for one of their micro-batch coffees. Grab one of the waffles made by Lt Waffle for perfect ride food while you're there. They have a variety of sweet and savoury flavour combinations, so there's a waffle for everyone.

Now it's time to hop on the bike for a mural tour. You're going to want to stop by both **Balmy Alley ❼** and **Clarion Alley ❽**. There are building-sized murals throughout the Mission, but these two alleys are not to be missed. The murals speak to the Latino heritage of the district, and while some are permanent, others are frequently painted over,

keeping the area fresh. Tours can be booked through **Precita Eyes ❾**, a community-based arts organization. Keep pedalling, there's more art to see. A few blocks east is **Southern Exposure ❿**, a blossoming place for visual artists since 1974. This nonprofit organization is a great place to check out emerging talent. For a different kind of art, make sure to stop into **Paxton Gate ⓫**. Filled with taxidermy, anatomical posters, plants galore and a kingdom of other oddities, this is where you'll find great gifts for your kookiest friends. And don't worry: like any good San Francisco store, they try to ethically source everything.

Assuming you've burned off the morning's sugar by now, it's time to enjoy one of the main food groups of the Mission: burritos. A delectable option is the 'Super Burrito' at **Taqueria Cancún ⓬**: bring cash and a hearty appetite. For the perfect picnic location, head over to **Mission Dolores Park ⓭** and grab a spot on the grass. You may even see locals relaxing with a bottle of wine, but that's not technically legal: BYOB at your own risk. While in the area, head around the corner to the actual **Mission Dolores ⓮** – it's the oldest building in San Francisco, founded by Spanish padres in 1776. Its 1.2 m (4 ft)-thick adobe walls have withstood more than a few earthquakes.

If the burrito sends you into an afternoon slump, cruise down Valencia St and re-caffeinate at **Ritual Coffee Roasters** ⑮, because it's time for some shopping. Stop by the **Pirate Supply Store** ⑯ for, you guessed it, pirating supplies, including but not limited to eye patches, hooks, and more. If your taste in fashion is more preppy than swashbuckling, stop by **Taylor Stitch** ⑰ to look sharp. If you see something you like, buy it: they may not make more. To spruce up your home, rather than yourself, stop by **Harrington Galleries** ⑱, one of the few remaining vintage and antiques shops in the Mission. There will certainly be pieces worth seeing, even if you don't see anything you want to take home on your bike.

The Mission is riddled with new, tantalizing restaurants, but one of the best experiences will be had at **Foreign Cinema** ⑲, where classic movies are projected onto the back wall, accompanied by a mix of Californian and Mediterranean cuisine. For the perfect thin-crust experience, you'll need to reserve your table well in advance at **Flour + Water** ⑳, a space designed by the same gentlemen behind Paxton Gate. After dinner, catch a show at the **Roxie Theater** ㉑, built in 1909 and now famous for screening avant-garde documentaries and classic horror films.

Or skip dinner and a show altogether for a different kind of night: ice cream and booze. Stop by **Humphry Slocombe** ㉒ for one of their unusual ice-cream flavours, from Peaches and Popcorn to Brown Butter. Then enjoy the rest of the evening at one of the Mission's many dive bars. Try **Royal Cuckoo** ㉓ for great cocktails, or **Zeitgeist** ㉔, a gritty biergarten with a cash-only, no-cameras policy.

REFUELLING

FOOD

Tamale Lady ㉕ is a cult favourite in the Mission
for her Mesoamerican specialities
Tartine Bakery ㉖ for the bread alone

DRINK

Monk's Kettle ㉗ is a neighbourhood joint
that should satisfy beer drinkers
Trick Dog ㉘ for the cocktail enthusiast

WIFI

Cafe La Boheme ㉙ for reliable Internet access and Moroccan beef stew

DOGPATCH & THE EMBARCADERO

A COAST OF CLASSICS

While you might not normally group the neighbourhoods of Dogpatch, the Embarcadero, North Beach and the Marina together, hitting them one after the other is a hill-free way to spend the day. Plus, the views just get better and better as you roll from the east side of the peninsula around the northeastern tip towards the Golden Gate Bridge. But first, get to Dogpatch before San Francisco eats it whole. New gastronomic hotspots are popping up in this neighbourhood like dandelions. Previously an industrial hub, it is quickly becoming the home to many artists and creative workspaces.

To start the day in Dogpatch, get a *beignet* from **Just For You ❶**. This was a local breakfast favourite long before the neighbourhood began to gain traction. For something small and packable, ride a block over to the can't-miss **Piccino Coffee Bar ❷** in the beautiful yellow Victorian building.

The owner is a cyclist, and the granola bars are jersey-friendly. You may find yourself back here later at its sister restaurant **Piccino** ❸: if you liked the granola, you'll love the homemade pasta. Just across the street is the messenger-bag shop and factory, **Rickshaw Bagworks** ❹. They're open Friday–Monday, and if you ask, you may get a factory tour. For brunch lovers, **The Ramp** ❺ has the view, but **Hard Knox Cafe** ❻ (technically a lunch spot) has the fried chicken and waffles.

Squeeze in a bit of art at the small but well-curated **Museum of Craft and Design** ❼. Or stop by **Pier 70** ❽, which is currently being renovated and often has pop-ups and events going on. But before pedalling out of Dogpatch, make sure to fill up on sweets, whether a funkily flavoured ice cream from **Mr and Mrs Miscellaneous** ❾, delicious confections from **Little Nib** ❿ or 'Bacon Crack' from the home base of **Nosh This** ⓫. Whatever you choose, your sweet tooth will be satisfied.

Ride along the coast through Mission Bay and past AT&T Park (see A Day On The Bike) to get on the Embarcadero. Your first stop will be the **Ferry Building Marketplace** ⓬. There's an outdoor farmers' market here three times a week, and plenty of indoor stalls where you can treat yourself to great coffee and pressed juices. Or grab a beer from the

Fort Point Beer Company ⑬ kiosk, brewed just over in Crissy Field (another Day On The Bike destination). The Ferry Building was in disrepair for decades, but is now one of the favourite spots in the whole of the city. For a superb Vietnamese meal, head to Charles Phan's **Slanted Door ⑭**. Or, if you didn't scratch the fried-chicken itch earlier at Hard Knox Cafe, head to Phan's newer place, **Hard Water ⑮**, known for its excellent New Orleans-style cuisine.

From the Ferry Building, ride into the city towards North Beach. This is the Little Italy of San Francisco, with plenty of great cafés, people-watching and a fair amount of adults-only entertainment. The area was the hotspot for the Beat Generation in the 1950s, and it's still home to many Italians. Those of a literary persuasion should stop by **City Lights Bookstore ⑯** for a helping of Beat poetry and literature, or swing by **Vesuvio ⑰** for a drink, a favourite hangout of Jack Kerouac. If coffee is your poison, **Caffe Trieste ⑱** was also a Beat hangout and makes some of the best espresso in the city.

Ride along Grant Ave for great boutiques and oddities shops, but make sure to swing by the whimsical **Schein & Schein ⑲**, a little off the beaten path, for maps, scientific illustrations and old brochures. For some local cuisine, get the oven-baked meatball foccacia sandwich at **Mario's Bohemian Cigar Store ⑳** (where you cannot get a cigar) or, for something non-Italian, swing by **Don Pisto's ㉑** for some seriously good tacos.

From here, you can ride back to the Bay to see Fisherman's Wharf, but be prepared for an uncomfortable number of tourists. This area is well covered in A Day On The Bike, but if there's anything worth seeing among the hokey attractions, it is perhaps the **Musée Mécanique ㉒**, an arcade with games that date back to the 1880s. And if this is your first time in California, you'll find an **In-N-Out Burger ㉓** here. Order your burger 'animal-style', then ride through the **Fort Mason ㉔** park area and head towards the Marina.

For a more local burger, **Mel's Drive-In ㉕** has you covered, and if you'd rather go gluten-, dairy- and meat-free, try **Seed + Salt ㉖**. Or if you just want more tacos, stop by **Chubby Noodle ㉗** for the Korean variety. Once you're full, ride it all off by checking out the majesty of the **Wave Organ ㉘**, built in 1986, and then ride along Crissy Field to the never-used defense location of **Fort Point ㉙**, just for the views.

REFUELLING

FOOD

Serpentine ㉚ for delicious, locally sourced food
Liguria Bakery ㉛ for the foccacia bread – if you
arrive early enough, that is

DRINK

Comstock Saloon ㉜ for the 'Barkeep's Whimsy' –
the bartender chooses your drink for you
Tipsy Pig ㉝ for brunch at a classic gastropub

WIFI

Cafe Capriccio ㉞ for plenty of outlets and big mugs

1 MILE = 4 MINS
1 KM

NORTH BEACH

EMBARCADERO

CENTRAL
WATERFRONT

DOWNTOWN & HAYES VALLEY

THE CHIC AND THE TECH

It may seem like San Francisco is an endless stream of quaint neighbourhoods – and it is – but there's also a lively downtown to experience. The geographical grouping of 'downtown' can include Union Square, Civic Center, Financial District, and more, depending on who you ask. For the sake of this guide, we'll also cover South of Market (SoMa), the Tenderloin and Hayes Valley. And to see it all, we'll do a bit of weaving between them.

Start off at one of San Francisco's coffee institutions: **Blue Bottle Coffee ❶** on Mint St or **Sightglass Coffee ❷** on 7th. Both will have you properly – if not overly – caffeinated. Ride through the Tenderloin and keep your eyes peeled for the incredible murals in this neighbourhood. The area gets a bad rap, but like the rest of San Francisco, there are plenty of people here trying to revitalize it, and it's full of cheap eats and great bars. Revitalize yourself with brunch at **Brenda's French Soul Food Kitchen ❸** or **Farmerbrown ❹**: you can't go wrong with either, but if you end up at the former, get the flight of *beignets*. Once you're full, pedal over to the **Asian Art Museum ❺**, the largest showcase for Asian art in the country. Across the way, you'll see the beautiful **San Francisco City Hall ❻**, as well as the **Public Library ❼**. For art of a different kind, head to **111 Minna Gallery ❽**, which turns into a dance club at night. And if galleries aren't your thing but you're looking for some beauty, try the **San Francisco Flower Mart ❾**. It can be a little chilly inside, but it smells fantastic.

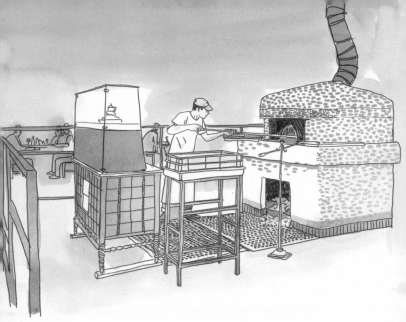

Just round the corner from 111 Minna is the Parisian paradise of **Trou Normand** ❿, inside the grand PacBell building. Enjoy a snack in the courtyard, but save some room, because a food extravaganza awaits at the **SoMa StrEat Food Park** ⓫. Not only will you find food truck upon food truck, but also beer, sangria and WiFi. You can power-lunch at **Tadich Grill** ⓬, the oldest restaurant in the city, or keep it simple by stopping by the garage door of **Una Pizza Napoletana** ⓭. The chef keeps it pretty simple, too: as he says, 'I bake pizza and ride bikes.'

Next, squeeze in a little retail therapy at the big department stores around **Union Square** ⓮, or the little boutiques along the former red-light district of **Maiden Lane** ⓯. Then lock up the bike and grab an afternoon drink at **Top of the Mark** ⓰ for a sky-high cocktail with a view, or go low-key with a brew at **City Beer Store** ⓱.

Alternatively, you could spend a whole day in the charming neighbourhood of Hayes Valley. Once overshadowed by the Central Freeway, the Loma Prieta earthquake in 1989 caused so much damage to the road that it had to be taken down, and Hayes Valley came to life.

Today, it's bustling with cool shops and great restaurants. Try brunch at **Boxing Room** ⑱ (the hushpuppies with pepper jelly are a must), or stroll along the streets to **Welcome Stranger** ⑲ for a mix of clothing and camping equipment or **Rand + Statler** ⑳ for high-end staples. The stores, along with clothing shop **Azalea** ㉑, were all launched by the same entrepreneurs, and the quality is consistent throughout.

Make sure to check out pop-up project Proxy, too – the shipping containers and parking lot, while not sounding glamorous, are the hub of this neighbourhood. It's home to **Ritual Coffee Roasters** ㉒ and **Smitten Ice Cream** ㉓, not to mention art exhibits, fitness meet-ups and outdoor movies. A popular evening ride in the city even ends here at **Biergarten** ㉔ (see also p. 40), as the proprietor has a long association with cycling. (You can find nods to the sport at his restaurant **Suppenküche** ㉕, just around the corner.)

To round out the day, have dinner at **Rich Table** ㉖, but be sure to make a reservation when you book your trip. It's a casual, often family-style restaurant, but this farm-to-table hotspot fills up fast, as it's just around the corner from **Davies Symphony Hall** ㉗, the **War Memorial Opera House** ㉘ and the new **SFJAZZ Center** ㉙. Catch a performance at any of these great venues, and then end the night at **Smuggler's Cove** ㉚. There's enough rum at this wonderful, kitschy mermaid-laden bar to convince anyone they're a pirate.

REFUELLING

FOOD

Marlowe ㉛ for Californian cuisine in SoMa – visit for the mouthwatering burgers alone
The Cavalier ㉜ for 'soldiers' wrapped in ham and cheese

DRINK

Powerhouse ㉝ for the free-spirited – or those who want to be
Two Sisters Bar and Books ㉞ for, you guessed it, booze and books

WIFI

Mercury Cafe ㉟ for the unique combo of pastries and PBR

FINANCIAL DISTRICT

MONTGOMERY ST
WASHINGTON ST

KEARNY ST

CALIFORNIA ST

PINE ST

BUSH ST

SPEAR ST

BEALE ST

12

16

PINE ST

BUSH ST

TAYLOR ST

GEARY BLVD

O'FARRELL ST

14

15

MARKET ST

MISSION ST

FREMONT ST

1ST ST

HOWARD ST

MAIN ST

8

10

2ND ST

FOLSOM ST

3RD ST

4

32

4TH ST

HOWARD ST

1

MISSION ST

5TH ST

FOLSOM ST

HARRISON ST

2ND ST

80

BRYANT ST

3RD ST

BRANNAN ST

6TH ST

7TH ST

SOUTH OF
MARKET

4TH ST

31

HOWARD ST

2

9TH ST

9

5TH ST

BRANNAN ST

KING ST

17

HARRISON ST

BRYANT ST

6TH ST

7TH ST

280

9TH ST

7TH ST

MISSION
BAY

CASTRO & HAIGHT-ASHBURY

FOR RAINBOWS AND LATE NIGHTS

There are more neighbourhoods than there are streets to contain them in San Francisco, and you'll really see that as you make your way through the Castro, Lower Haight, Haight-Ashbury, Duboce Triangle, Fillmore District, Western Addition, Alamo Square, Divis, North of the Panhandle (NoPa), Japantown, Lower Pacific Heights and Pacific Heights. It's best to just check out all the great places in these areas, and leave it to the locals to define what area that is. Two uncontested neighbourhoods, however, are the Castro and Haight-Ashbury, emblematic strongholds of the movements that defined San Francisco's rise.

The Castro, where gay pride blossomed, is gayer (in both senses of the word) than ever. Walk around and you'll see rainbows everywhere – even the crosswalks are painted in rainbow colours. On Castro St itself, keep an eye out for the bronze plaques on the **Rainbow Honor Walk ❶**, which pays homage to some of the heroes in the LBGTQ community. For food, skip the circus at Fisherman's Wharf and get your clam chowder-fix at the counter at the **Anchor Oyster Bar ❷**, or make a reservation at **Frances ❸** for a heightened soup experience. And for a classic Castro evening, stop into **Moby Dick ❹** for pool, pinball and a welcoming crowd, or try **The Cafe ❺** if you're looking to dance.

North of the Castro is Haight-Ashbury, home of the Summer of Love in 1967 and now home to plenty of boutiques and organic restaurants. No trip to San Francisco is complete without a photo of the **iconic street signs ❻** at the corner of Haight and Ashbury. Once you've snapped your picture, lock up your bike and walk along the main drag of Haight St. You can fulfil all your vintage clothing needs at **Held Over ❼** and **Wasteland ❽**, or for bedroom vintage, check out **Dollhouse Bettie ❾**. And for what might as well be vintage, look through one of the biggest CD collections in the world at **Amoeba Music ❿**. If you've worked up an appetite, **Sparrow ⓫** is great place for wine and cheese, or enjoy a long, Caribbean-paced meal at **Cha Cha Cha ⓬**. Leave a little room for cocktails, because both **Aub Zam Zam ⓭** and **Alembic ⓮** aim to impress.

Next, head east and ride up to the top of **Buena Vista Park ⓯**, the oldest park in the city. It's small, but packs quite a view. Just a few blocks east of the park, you'll find yourself in the NoPa/Western Addition area. Here, you'll discover great shops like **Rare Device ⓰** (perfect for gifts) and **Cookin' ⓱** (perfect for kitchen gifts, and really just lovely for anyone who enjoys a good pan). For food, **Nopa ⓲** is a unique treat in a city where most kitchens close at 10pm – it's open until 1am, serving earthy dishes to wash down with cocktails. You may also want to stop by Nopa's offshoot, **Nopalito ⓳** for rustic Mexican fare. And no trip to NoPa would be complete without a stop into quintessential San Francisco spot, **The Mill ⓴**, a joint effort from Four Barrel Coffee and Josey Baker Bread, where toast is the item to get. While toast may not seem that exciting, just try the Cinnamon or Birthday varieties to see what all the fuss is about.

Riding through this area will take you to the Fillmore District, formerly known as the 'Harlem of the West' for its music. You can still see a great show at the aptly named legendary venue **The Fillmore ㉑**, too.

For a low-key meal before a show, stop into **Fat Angel Food & Libation** ㉒, or make a reservation at Michelin-starred **State Bird Provisions** ㉓ for small plates with bold flavours. If you're showing up on the night, get there early and enjoy a drink at **The Social Study** ㉔ while you wait for your table. You could also amble across the street to Japantown to check out the **Sundance Kabuki Cinema** ㉕, with its own cafés and even a bar. One more block over, and you'll find yourself in a mall of colourful J-Pop stores. Stop into LA-transplant **Ramen Yamadaya** ㉖, where the *tonkatsu* is can't-miss.

If you're just looking to ogle, ride around Pacific Heights: the architecture is grand and the attitude is refined. The neighbourhood is also home to perfect post-ride stop: **b. patisserie** ㉗, creators of the flaky, buttery piece of heaven known as a *kouign-amann*. No other croissant comes close.

REFUELLING

FOOD

Thep Phanom ㉘ in the Lower Haight for the 'angel wings'
Pizzeria Delfina ㉙ for reliably good pizza

DRINK

Mad Dog in the Fog ㉚ has the best beer selection in the city
Maven ㉛ to try the Hometown Vixen

WIFI

At Ethiopian eatery Oasis Cafe ㉜, you'll always find a seat

SUNSET & GOLDEN GATE PARK

A BRIDGE IN THE FOG

The westside of the peninsula, unfazed by hipness or trends, is one of the most beautiful, with sweeping views of the ocean, a salty crispness in the air and fog rolling into the city. It's here that you'll find the quieter neighbourhoods, filled with shops and restaurants that are frequented not because they're cool, but because they're great. Ride around **Lake Merced** ❶, before checking out the views at **Fort Funston** ❷. You'll spot **San Francisco Zoo** ❸ on your right, then hop on the bike path that runs parallel to the Great Highway. These outerlands were sand dunes before being developed, and the highway and path remain strewn with sand.

In the Outer Sunset neighbourhood, you'll find several hubs of goodness, but make sure to ride along Noriega and Judah Sts. On Noriega, you'll find fresh fruit and homemade peanut butter at **Noriega Produce ❹**, and Sightglass coffee and $5-sandwiches (about £4) at **Devil's Teeth Baking Company ❺**. If you're here later in the day, **Pizza Place on Noriega ❻** and the Korean late-night hole-in-the-wall **Toyose ❼** will do the trick. A few more blocks up the coast, turn onto Judah St. Proper caffeine kicks can be found at **Java Beach Café ❽** and the impressively decorated **Trouble Coffee ❾**. The latter is also famous for starting the 'toast movement', so give the cinnamon toast a try while you're there.

If juice and smoothies are your thing, stop into **Judahlicious ❿** for a great selection. And make time for a bit of shopping at **General Store ⓫**, where you'll find exactly the kind of artisanal goods with the beachy/desert vibe you expect from California. If you're having dinner here, make your destination the wood-clad **Outerlands ⓬**: from porridge to pork, there's no bad way to warm up in this chilly neighbourhood. Cap off the cosy feeling with a bonfire at **Ocean Beach ⓭** – just be prepared for some sandy bikes.

A little further inland and uphill, grab a brew at the latest Outer Sunset hotspot, **Sunset Reservoir Brewing Company ⓮**. Once you hit 19th Ave, you're riding into the Inner Sunset. This area is home to the San Francisco campus of the University of California, and has a bit of that small college-town feel. Hop off the bike to check out the **16th Ave Tiled Steps ⓯**, which imitate a beautiful path from sea to sky. Walk up all 163 mosaic-tiled steps and earn your stop at **San Tung ⓰** for some of the best chicken wings in the city.

North of Sunset is Golden Gate Park (see A Day On The Bike). Save some time to spend here; it's over 1,000 acres and offers not only great cycling, but great stopping, too. The **California Academy of Sciences ⓱** has an aquarium, natural-history museum and planetarium, all in the same compound. Also in this area of the park you'll find the **De Young Fine Arts Museum ⓲** and the **Japanese Tea Garden ⓳**. Further along John F. Kennedy Dr is the **Conservatory of Flowers ⓴**, the oldest Victorian greenhouse in the Western Hemisphere. Ride around the whole park and if you have any trouble, **Freewheel Bike Shop ㉑** is just outside on Hayes St for any tune-ups you might need. At the other end of the park, once you've worked up an appetite, lock up the bikes for a bite at the airy **Park Chalet Garden Restaurant ㉒**.

North of the park is the Richmond District, a foggy haven of residential streets separating Golden Gate Park from the Presidio. But there are still some sweet places to duck into here. For the interiors-inclined, visit **Mixed Nuts** ㉓, which is stocked to the ceiling with vintage treasures from the 1940s to the '60s. More transportable oddities and gifts can be found at the enormous **Park Life** ㉔, both a gallery for emerging artists and a store full of design-inspired goodies. And if you still haven't satisfied your burrito itch in San Francisco, stop into **Gordo Taqueria** ㉕ for the super-sized carne asada burrito.

From here, it's into the Presidio. A former military base, you'll still find many of the old buildings here. The **Presidio Social Club** ㉖, which hosts an excellent cocktail hour, is even housed in what used to be barracks. Ride around the park just to see the buildings, and cap the day off with a pedal over the Golden Gate Bridge.

REFUELLING

FOOD
Heartbaker ㉗ for their special *bombolini*, custard-filled doughnuts
Fiorella ㉘ for pizza better than it has a right to be

DRINK
The Riptide ㉙ has a great fireplace for warming cycle-weary toes by
Colourful Mexican eatery **Padrecito** ㉚ for cocktails

WIFI
Cafe Enchante ㉛ has plenty of room for all your laptop needs

VICENTE ST

36TH AV

SLOAT BLVD

OCEAN AV

GREAT HIGHWAY

3 ◐

LAKE MERCED BLVD

1 ◑

2 ◐

JOHN MUIR DR

SEA

GEARY BLVD

BALBOA ST 28

FULTON ST

22 ⑂

LINCOLN WAY

8 ⑂ 12 ⑂ 10 ⑂ JUDAH ST

13 ◐ 9 ⑂ 11 ⑂

SUNSET BLVD

OUTER SU

5 ⑂ 7 ⑂ NORIEGA

6 ⑂ 4 ◐

GREAT HIGHWAY

SUNSET BLVD

29 ⑂ TARAVAL ST

VICENTE ST

RACING & TRAINING

San Francisco is synonymous with cycling. It's estimated that there are over 80,000 bike trips made in the city each day and, given the grades of so many of the roads, nearly every ride could be considered a training ride. But some of the best riding is just outside of the city: the San Francisco Bay Area is home to several quintessential American rides, including crossing the Golden Gate Bridge, riding up Mt Tamalpais, and exploring the Marin Headlands. The modern mountain bike is even credited as being designed in Marin County in the 1970s.

In addition to mountain bikers, commuters, tourists on cruisers and plenty of fixies, you'll also find a whole bunch of road racers here. Northern California hosts some of the best road races in the state, not to mention bike-friendly weather for most of the year. While racing in the States has a long way to go before reaching European levels, there's still a history of racing in San Francisco. **Il Giro de San Francisco** began in 1975 (then known as the San Francisco Gran Prix) and is still happening today; its most famous winner, Greg LeMond, won the crit in both 1979 and 1980. And the inaugural **Tour of California** began in San Francisco in 2006, with stages held in the Bay Area nearly every year since. If racing is your bag, there's no shortage of ways to rack up points in this part of California.

If you're looking to join a ride while in town, consider hopping on the **Stammtisch Ride**, held every Thursday evening during daylight savings time, beginning at the **Rapha Cycle Club** (see p. 46) and ending two hours later at Biergarten (see p. 25) in Hayes Valley. What better way to head towards the weekend than with a ride that begins with an espresso and ends with a beer? There are also open Saturday rides held at the Cycle Club, which you can sign up for online. For a competitive training ride, try the Roasters Ride, which meets every Saturday at 8am at the Golden Gate Bridge South Parking Lot. It takes you out to Point Reyes Station, for a total of 129 km (80 miles). If you want something more social, Scotty's Ride leaves from the Golden Gate Bridge Pavilion at 8:30am on Saturdays, taking a route similar to the Roasters Ride, but stops for food at **Bovine** in Point Reyes Station.

Of course, many of the bike shops in the city also host their own rides, so call around to see where the latest start and finish points land you. And if you'd rather see the sights for yourself, there is no shortage of must-ride routes. You can ride every street in San Francisco proper, but the best rides are across the Golden Gate Bridge. The classic ride is the **Hawk Hill Loop**, best done at dawn to catch an incredible sunrise and some of the best views of the city. It's a short ride, but one of the most travelled.

For a ride (or climb) through the trees, try the **Alpine Dam Loop**. You'll wind through towns, pedal up to Mt Tam, and find yourself rewarded with some epic descents. When it comes to riding in Marin County, the Alpine Dam Loop is second to none. After meandering

through a handful of friendly towns, the road turns uphill – and that's when this loop really begins to set itself apart. This ride is all about pleasure and pain, combining fantastic views and scenery with challenging climbs and wicked descents. From the bridge, this route is a little over 85 km (53 miles). For something a little less steep, try the route known as **Paradise Loop**. This will put you on quieter roads and is suited to all skill levels – and will take you through the charming towns of Sausalito and Tiburon, as well.

No matter where you ride in the area, there are plenty of top-notch bike shops to help get you set for adventure. If you're just looking for a kit upgrade, try the Rapha Cycle Club (see p. 40) or **Bespoke Cycles**. The latter also offers one of the best bike fits in the city, if you find your measurements off after unpacking your bicycle. For excellent customer service, you can't go wrong with **Huckleberry Bicycles**. Not only are they good to their customers, but they give back to the community and to the San Francisco Bicycle Coalition (see p. 45), as well. **Mojo Bicycle Cafe** is a worthy stop – and why wouldn't it be? You can have a beer while you get your bike fixed. And if you find your bike needing a tune-up after the ride, head over to **City + County Bicycle Co.**, where you'll find yourself treated with the perfect sugar fix: an ice-cold Mexican Coke.

ESSENTIAL BIKE INFO

Bikes are everywhere in San Francisco, along with cars, trains, skateboarders, longboarders, pedestrians, scooters, and everything in between. Keep your wits (and your locks) about you. There are bike paths and lanes that can all make getting around the city a little bit easier, so plan your routes ahead of time and watch out for signs and lanes before you end up doing a walk-a-bike up a 30 per cent grade.

ETIQUETTE

You'll find every type of two-wheeler in San Francisco, many doing whatever they please. Here are a few tips to keep you safe and law-abiding:

- You'll see a lot of locals forgoing the laws here, but remember that pedestrians have the right of way and bikes are required to stop at stop signs and red lights, just like cars.
- Taking the lane is legal here, even when there's a dedicated bike lane. If it feels safer to be in the flow of traffic, signal and merge into the lane.
- Unless you're under the age of 13, it is illegal to ride on the sidewalk.
- Given the amount of cyclists here, don't be surprised if a few pass you. Passing on the left is always the way to go.
- Getting 'doored' is not uncommon. Even if there is a bike lane, do not assume the cars parked next to it are checking for you.

SAFETY

Bikes are everywhere in San Francisco, but it's still best to use caution when navigating the cars and public transit. Here are a few more tips to keep you safe on the hills:

- This is a city of stop signs. It can be tempting to cruise through after the fourth stop sign with no vehicles, but it's tempting for people going the other direction, too.
- Watch out for tracks on the road – you don't want to get a wheel stuck. Many of the painted lanes will take you on the angle to pass over safely.
- If riding with headphones, keep one ear free. It's the law.

- You'll see 'Bike Route' signs posted around the city – these are not reliable for following a route, nor are those roads treated any differently by drivers.
- San Francisco is famous for its fog. If you can, ride with lights.
- Use extra caution around Fisherman's Wharf, the Presidio and the Golden Gate Bridge, as these areas are littered with novices on cruisers riding for scenery, not watts.

SECURITY

Bike theft is prevalent in San Francisco. The *San Francisco Bay Guardian* estimates that over two thousand bikes are stolen in the city each year, so don't leave any bike unlocked or unattended. Think about using two locks and securing the wheels together, and always go with a U-lock over a cable lock. Seats, pumps, saddlebags, and the like are all at risk, so take your bike inside at night to ensure it's all in one piece in the morning. And make sure to write down the serial number on your bike: if it's stolen, that's the best way to track it down. Report any stolen bikes to the **SFPD Anti Bike Theft** unit: @sfpdbiketheft.

FINDING YOUR WAY

The **San Francisco Bicycle Coalition** provides an incredibly detailed map of the best walking and biking routes in the city. Not only does the map show you the grades of the streets, but it also includes the locations of bike shops and what type of bikeway is on each street. Of course, Google Maps and SF's own **BikeMapper** are great on-the-go services, too.

Finding your way without tech is easy, too, given that the bike lanes are often painted bright green, marked with 'sharrows' (shared-lane marking; arrows and a bicycle painted on the ground), or sometimes will be indicated by street signs, especially in the case of the Wiggle. The most popular bike thoroughfares in the city are the Wiggle, Valencia St, Polk St, Fell and Oak Sts, and 17th St. Make your way to one of those, and there will be hundreds of fellow cyclists to follow. Or, worst case scenario, ride up a hill and look for the bridges to reorient yourself.

CITY BIKES AND BIKE HIRE

San Francisco's **Bay Area Bike Share** has been used over 800,000 times to date, but so far there are only stations in the northeastern portion of the peninsula. If you'd like to try it for yourself, look for the mint-coloured bikes, kept at solar-powered electronic kiosks. There you can swipe your credit card for all types of memberships. A day pass is only $9 (or just over £7), and so long as each trip during that day is 30 minutes or less, there's no additional cost. Check out the website for more details.

If you're looking to rent a high-end road or mountain bike, make sure to do so well in advance of your trip. Selection can be dire or nonexistent at some shops during certain times of the year. If you're a member of the Rapha Cycle Club (see p. 40), you can reserve a bicycle at their San Francisco location. If not, check out the Columbus Ave location of **Blazing Saddles**. Make sure to call, as their online selection is not always reflective of what they have in the shop. Another option when looking for a high-end bike is **Black Sheep Bike Rental**, but make sure to call ahead and reserve. Major perk: Black Sheep will deliver the bike to your hotel.

OTHER PUBLIC TRANSPORT

You might just picture cable cars when imaging transportation, San Francisco-style, but it's more comprehensive than that these days. You can get wherever you need to go by using the **Muni** (the city's network of buses, cable cars and light rails) and **BART** (officially Bay Area Rapid Transit, and more of a regional commuter train). Both Muni buses and BART are bike-friendly, but read up on the rules first. And beware, historic streetcars, cable cars, even the Muni light rail, don't have bike racks and thus don't allow bicycles. The city is still only 11 km (7 miles) across – you can likely ride wherever you need to go. San Francisco is also the home of the headquarters of the biggest ride-sharing apps, so if a personal driver is more your style, make sure to request a car large enough to put a bike in the back.

TRAVELLING TO SAN FRANCISCO WITH BIKES

If you are travelling internationally to San Francisco with a bike, be prepared to pay upwards of about £240 ($300) round trip to check your bike on the plane. Smaller airlines like Southwest, JetBlue and Frontier offer lower prices than the larger airlines, but fees still add up. **San Francisco International Airport** is about 24 km (15 miles) from the city, and the easiest (and cheapest) way to get to it with your bike is to take BART. The station at SFO is in the International Terminal, but you can take the free **AirTran** from all terminals directly there. If you're flying into **Oakland International Airport**, there's a BART station there now, too.

LINKS AND ADDRESSES

111 MINNA GALLERY
111 Minna St,
San Francisco, CA 94105
111minnagallery.com

16TH AVE TILED STEPS
16th Ave,
San Francisco, CA 94122
tiledsteps.org

ALEMBIC
1725 Haight St,
San Francisco, CA 94117
alembicbar.com

AMOEBA MUSIC
1855 Haight St,
San Francisco, CA 94117
amoeba.com

ANCHOR OYSTER BAR
579 Castro St,
San Francisco, CA 94114
anchoroysterbar.com

ASIAN ART MUSEUM
200 Larkin St,
San Francisco, CA 94102
asianart.org

AT&T PARK
24 Willie Mays Plaza,
San Francisco, CA 94107
sanfrancisco.giants.mlb.com/sf/
ballpark

AUB ZAM ZAM
1633 Haight St,
San Francisco, CA 94117

AZALEA
411 Hayes St,
San Francisco, CA 94102
azaleasf.com

BALMY ALLEY
50 Balmy St,
San Francisco, CA 94110
balmyalley.com

BAR BOCCE
1250 Bridgeway,
Sausalito, CA 94965
barbocce.com

BAY BRIDGE
baybridgeinfo.org

BERNAL HEIGHTS PARK
Bernal Heights Blvd,
San Francisco, CA 94110
sfrecpark.org/destination/
bernal-heights-park

BIERGARTEN
424 Octavia St,
San Francisco, CA 94102
biergartensf.com

BLUE BOTTLE COFFEE
66 Mint St,
San Francisco, CA 94103
bluebottlecoffee.com

BOVINE
11315 CA-1,
Point Reyes Station, CA 94956
bovinebakeryptreyes.com

BOXING ROOM
399 Grove St,
San Francisco, CA 94102
boxingroom.com

B. PATISSERIE
2821 California St,
San Francisco, CA 94115
bpatisserie.com

**BRENDA'S FRENCH
SOUL FOOD KITCHEN**
652 Polk St,
San Francisco, CA 94102
frenchsoulfood.com

BUENA VISTA PARK
Buena Vista and Haight St,
San Francisco, CA 94117
sfrecpark.org/destination/
buena-vista-park

CAFE CAPRICCIO
2200 Mason St,
San Francisco, CA 94133
cafecapricciosanfrancisco.com

CAFE ENCHANTE
6157 Geary Blvd,
San Francisco, CA 94121
facebook.com/Café-
Enchante-156384367771474

CAFE LA BOHEME
3318 24th St,
San Francisco, CA 94110
cafelabohemesanfrancisco.com

CAFFE TRIESTE
601 Vallejo St,
San Francisco, CA 94133
caffetrieste.com

**CALIFORNIA ACADEMY OF
SCIENCES**
55 Music Concourse Dr,
San Francisco, CA 94118
calacademy.org

CHA CHA CHA
1801 Haight St,
San Francisco, CA 94117
cha3.com

CHUBBY NOODLE
1310 Grant Ave,
San Francisco, CA 94133
chubbynoodle.com

CITY BEER STORE
1168 Folsom St, #101,
San Francisco, CA 94103
citybeerstore.com

CITY LIGHTS BOOKSTORE
261 Columbus Ave,
San Francisco, CA 94133
citylights.com

CLARION ALLEY
90 Clarion Alley,
San Francisco, CA 94110
clarionalleymuralproject.org

COIT TOWER
1 Telegraph Hill Blvd,
San Francisco, CA 94133
sfrecpark.org/destination/telegraph-
hill-pioneer-park/coit-tower

COMSTOCK SALOON
155 Columbus Ave,
San Francisco, CA 94133
comstocksaloon.com

CONSERVATORY OF FLOWERS
100 John F. Kennedy Dr,
San Francisco, CA 94118
conservatoryofflowers.org

COOKIN'
339 Divisadero St,
San Francisco, CA 94117

CRAFTSMAN AND WOLVES
746 Valencia St,
San Francisco, CA 94110
craftsman-wolves.com

CRISSY FIELD
Golden Gate National
Recreation Area,
San Francisco, CA 94129
parksconservancy.org/visit/park-
sites/crissy-field

DAVIES SYMPHONY HALL
201 Van Ness Ave,
San Francisco, CA 94102
sfsymphony.org

DE YOUNG FINE ARTS MUSEUM
50 Hagiwara Tea Garden Dr,
San Francisco, CA 94118
deyoung.famsf.org

**DEVIL'S TEETH BAKING
COMPANY**
3876 Noriega St,
San Francisco, CA 94122
devilsteethbakingcompany.com

DOLLHOUSE BETTIE
1641 Haight St,
San Francisco, CA 94117
dollhousebettie.com

DON PISTO'S
510 Union St,
San Francisco, CA 94133
donpistos.com

DYNAMO DONUT AND COFFEE
2760 24th St,
San Francisco, CA 94110
dynamodonut.com

EXPLORATORIUM
Pier 15, The Embarcadero
and Green St.,
San Francisco, CA 94111
exploratorium.edu

FARMERBROWN
Hotel Metropolis,
25 Mason St,
San Francisco, CA 94102
farmerbrownsf.com

FAT ANGEL FOOD & LIBATION
1740 O'Farrell St,
San Francisco, CA 94115
fatangelsf.com

**FERRY BUILDING +
MARKETPLACE**
1 Ferry Bldg,
San Francisco, CA 94111
ferrybuildingmarketplace.com

FIORELLA
2339 Clement St,
San Francisco, CA 94121
fiorella-sf.com

FISHERMAN'S WHARF
fishermanswharf.org

FLOUR + WATER
2401 Harrison St,
San Francisco, CA 94110
flourandwater.com

FOREIGN CINEMA
2534 Mission St,
San Francisco, CA 94110
foreigncinema.com

FORT FUNSTON
Golden Gate National
Recreation Area,
Fort Funston Rd,
San Francisco, CA 94132
nps.gov/goga/planyourvisit/
fortfunston

FORT MASON
Golden Gate National
Recreation Area,
Landmark Building C,
2 Marina Blvd,
San Francisco, CA 94123
fortmason.org

FORT POINT
Long Ave and Marine Dr,
San Francisco, CA 94129
nps.gov/fopo

FORT POINT BEER COMPANY
Kiosk, 1 Ferry Bldg,
San Francisco, CA 94111
fortpointbeer.com

FRANCES
3870 17th St,
San Francisco, CA 94114
frances-sf.com

GENERAL STORE
4035 Judah St,
San Francisco, CA 94122
shop-generalstore.com

**GHIRARDELLI CHOCOLATE
COMPANY**
Ghirardelli Square,
900 North Point St, #52,
San Francisco, CA 94109
sftodo.com/ghiradelli-square

GOLDEN GATE BRIDGE
goldengatebridge.org/visitors

GOLDEN GATE PARK
San Francisco, CA 94122
sfrecpark.org/destination/
golden-gate-park

GORDO TAQUERIA
5450 Geary Blvd,
San Francisco, CA 94121
gordotaqueria.co

HARD KNOX CAFE
2526 3rd St,
San Francisco, CA 94107
hardknoxcafe.com

HARD WATER
Pier 3, The Embarcadero,
San Francisco, CA 94105
hardwaterbar.com

HARRINGTON GALLERIES
599 Valencia St,
San Francisco, CA 94110
harringtongalleries.com

HEARTBAKER
1408 Clement St,
San Francisco, CA 94118
theheartbaker.com

HELD OVER
1543 Haight St,
San Francisco, CA 94117
facebook.com/Heldovervintage

HUMPHRY SLOCOMBE
2790 Harrison St,
San Francisco, CA 94110
humphryslocombe.com

IN-N-OUT BURGER
Anchorage Square,
333 Jefferson St,
San Francisco, CA 94133
locations.in-n-out.com/154

JAPANESE TEA GARDEN
75 Hagiwara Tea Garden Dr,
San Francisco, CA 94102
japaneseteagardensf.com

JAVA BEACH CAFÉ
1396 La Playa St,
San Francisco, CA 94122
javabeachcafe.com

JUDAHLICIOUS
3906 Judah St,
San Francisco, CA 94122
judahlicious.com

JUST FOR YOU
732 22nd St,
San Francisco, CA 94107
justforyoucafe.com

LAKE MERCED
Skyline Blvd and Harding Rd,
San Francisco, CA 94132
sfrecpark.org/destination/
lake-merced-park

LA MEXICANA
2804 24th St,
San Francisco, CA 94110

LAPPERT'S
689 Bridgeway,
Sausalito, CA 94965
lapperts.com

LA TAQUERIA
2889 Mission St,
San Francisco, CA 94110

LA VICTORIA
2937 24th St,
San Francisco, CA 94110
lavictoriabakery.com

LIGURIA BAKERY
1700 Stockton St,
San Francisco, CA 94133

LINEA CAFFE
3417 18th St,
San Francisco, CA 94110
lineacaffe.com

LITTLE NIB
807 22nd St,
San Francisco, CA 94107
littlenib.com

LOMBARD ST
Lombard St,
San Francisco, CA 94133

MAD DOG IN THE FOG
530 Haight St,
San Francisco, CA 94117
themaddoginthefog.com

MAIDEN LANE
San Francisco, CA 94108
maiden-lane.com

MAMA'S
1701 Stockton St,
San Francisco, CA 94133
mamas-sf.com

**MARIO'S BOHEMIAN CIGAR
STORE**
566 Columbus Ave,
San Francisco, CA 94133

MARLOWE
500 Brannan St,
San Francisco, CA 94107
marlowesf.com

MAVEN
598 Haight St,
San Francisco, CA 94117
maven-sf.com

MEL'S DRIVE-IN
2165 Lombard St,
San Francisco, CA 94123
melsdrive-in.com

MERCURY CAFE
201 Octavia St,
San Francisco, CA 94102
mercurycafe.net

MISSION DOLORES
3321 16th St,
San Francisco, CA 94114
missiondolores.org

MISSION DOLORES PARK
Dolores and 19th Sts,
San Francisco, CA 94114
sfrecpark.org/destination/
mission-dolores-park

MIXED NUTS
3243 Balboa St,
San Francisco, CA 94121
shopmixednuts.com

MOBY DICK
4049 18th St,
San Francisco, CA 94114
mobydicksf.com

MONK'S KETTLE
3141 16th St,
San Francisco, CA 94103
monkskettle.com

MR AND MRS MISCELLANEOUS
699 22nd St,
San Francisco, CA 94107

MUSÉE MÉCANIQUE
Pier 45, A,
San Francisco, CA 94133
museemecaniquesf.com

MUSEUM OF CRAFT AND DESIGN
2569 3rd St,
San Francisco, CA 94107
sfmcd.org

NOPA
560 Divisadero St,
San Francisco, CA 94117
nopasf.com

NOPALITO
306 Broderick St,
San Francisco, CA 94117
nopalitosf.com

NORIEGA PRODUCE
3821 Noriega St,
San Francisco, CA 94122

NOSH THIS
Ste 326, 2325 3rd St,
San Francisco, CA 94107
noshthis.com

OASIS CAFE
901 Divisadero St,
San Francisco, CA 94115
oasiscafesf.com

OCEAN BEACH
parksconservancy.org/visit/park-
sites/ocean-beach

OLD MILL PARK
Throckmorton Ave,
Mill Valley, CA 94941
millvalleyrecreation.org/facilities/
community_center/boyle_n_old_
mill_park

OUTERLANDS
4001 Judah St,
San Francisco, CA 94122
outerlandssf.com

PADRECITO
901 Cole St,
San Francisco, CA 94117
padrecitosf.com

PALACE OF FINE ARTS THEATRE
3301 Lyon St,
San Francisco, CA 94123
palaceoffinearts.org

PAN LIDO SALVADORENO
3147 22nd St,
San Francisco, CA 94110

**PARK CHALET GARDEN
RESTAURANT**
1000 Great Hwy,
San Francisco, CA 94121
parkchalet.com

PARK LIFE
220 Clement St,
San Francisco, CA 94118
parklifestore.com

PAXTON GATE
824 Valencia St,
San Francisco, CA 94110
paxtongate.com

PHILZ COFFEE
3101 24th St,
San Francisco, CA 94110
philzcoffee.com

PICCINO + PICCINO COFFEE BAR
1001 Minnesota St,
San Francisco, CA 94107
piccino.com

PIER 39
Beach St and The Embarcadero,
San Francisco, CA 94133
pier39.com

PIER 70
420 22nd St,
San Francisco, CA 94107
pier70sf.com

PIRATE SUPPLY STORE
826 Valencia St,
San Francisco, CA 94110
826valencia.org/store

PIZZA PLACE ON NORIEGA
3901 Noriega St,
San Francisco, CA 94122
pizzaplacesf.com

PIZZERIA DELFINA
2406 California St,
San Francisco, CA 94115
pizzeriadelfina.com

POWERHOUSE
1347 Folsom St,
San Francisco, CA 94103
powerhousebar.com

PRECITA EYES
2981 24th St,
San Francisco, CA 94110
precitaeyes.org

PRESIDIO
Presidio of San Francisco,
San Francisco, CA 94129
nps.gov/prsf/index

PRESIDIO SOCIAL CLUB
563 Ruger St,
San Francisco, CA 94129
presidiosocialclub.com

RAINBOW HONOR WALK
584 Castro St, #113,
San Francisco, CA 94114
rainbowhonorwalk.org

RAMEN YAMADAYA
1728 Buchanan St,
San Francisco, CA 94115
ramen-yamadaya.com

RAND + STATLER
425 Hayes St,
San Francisco, CA 94102
randandstatler.com

RARE DEVICE
600 Divisadero St,
San Francisco, CA 94117
raredevice.net

RICH TABLE
199 Gough St,
San Francisco, CA 94102
richtablesf.com

RICKSHAW BAGWORKS
904 22nd St,
San Francisco, CA 94107
rickshawbags.com

RITUAL COFFEE ROASTERS
• 1026 Valencia St,
  San Francisco, CA 94110
• 432b Octavia St,
  San Francisco, CA 94102
ritualroasters.com

ROXIE THEATER
3117 16th St,
San Francisco, CA 94103
roxie.com

ROYAL CUCKOO
3202 Mission St,
San Francisco, CA 94110
royalcuckoo.com

**SAN FRANCISCO BOTANICAL
GARDEN**
1199 9th Ave,
San Francisco, CA 94122
sfbotanicalgarden.org

SAN FRANCISCO CITY HALL
1 Dr Carlton B. Goodlett Pl,
San Francisco, CA 94102
sfgov.org/cityhall

SAN FRANCISCO FLOWER MART
640 Brannan St,
San Francisco, CA 94107
sanfranciscoflowermart.com

**SAN FRANCISCO PUBLIC
LIBRARY**
100 Larkin St,
San Francisco, CA 94102
sfpl.org

SAN FRANCISCO ZOO
1 Zoo Rd,
San Francisco, CA 94132
sfzoo.org

SAN TUNG
1031 Irving St,
San Francisco, CA 94122

SCHEIN & SCHEIN
1435 Grant Ave,
San Francisco, CA 94133
scheinandschein.com

SEED + SALT
2240 Chestnut St,
San Francisco, CA 94123
seedandsalt.com

SERPENTINE
2495 3rd St,
San Francisco, CA 94107
serpentinesf.com

SFJAZZ CENTER
201 Franklin St,
San Francisco, CA 94102
sfjazz.org

SIGHTGLASS COFFEE
270 7th St,
San Francisco, CA 94103
sightglasscoffee.com

SLANTED DOOR
1 Ferry Building #3,
San Francisco, CA 94111
slanteddoor.com

SMITTEN ICE CREAM
432 Octavia St, #1a,
San Francisco, CA 94102
smittenicecream.com

SMUGGLER'S COVE
650 Gough St,
San Francisco, CA 94102
smugglerscovesf.com

SOMA STREAT FOOD PARK
428 11th St,
San Francisco, CA 94103
somastreatfoodpark.com

SOUTHERN EXPOSURE
3030 20th St,
San Francisco, CA 94110
soex.org

SPARROW
1640 Haight St,
San Francisco, CA 94117
sparrowbarandkitchen.com

STATE BIRD PROVISIONS
1529 Fillmore St,
San Francisco, CA 94115
statebirdsf.com

SUNDANCE KABUKI CINEMA
1881 Post St,
San Francisco, CA 94115
sundancecinemas.com

SUNSET RESERVOIR BREWING COMPANY
1735 Noriega St,
San Francisco, CA 94122
sunsetbeersf.com

SUPPENKÜCHE
525 Laguna St,
San Francisco, CA 94102
suppenkuche.com

TADICH GRILL
240 California St,
San Francisco, CA 94111
tadichgrill.com

TAMALE LADY
Mission St,
San Francisco, CA 94102

TAQUERIA CANCÚN
2288 Mission St,
San Francisco, CA 94110

TARTINE BAKERY
600 Guerrero St,
San Francisco, CA 94110
tartinebakery.com

TAYLOR STITCH
383 Valencia St,
San Francisco, CA 94103
taylorstitch.com

THE CAFE
2369 Market St,
San Francisco, CA 94114
cafesf.com

THE CAVALIER
360 Jessie St,
San Francisco, CA 94103
thecavaliersf.com

THE FILLMORE
1805 Geary Blvd,
San Francisco, CA 94115
thefillmore.com

THE MILL
736 Divisadero St,
San Francisco, CA 94117
themillsf.com

THEP PHANOM
400 Waller St,
San Francisco, CA 94117
thepphanom.com

THE RAMP
855 Terry A. Francois Blvd,
San Francisco, CA 94158
theramprestaurant.com

THE RIPTIDE
3639 Taraval St,
San Francisco, CA 94116
riptidesf.com

THE SOCIAL STUDY
1795 Geary Blvd,
San Francisco, CA 94115
thesocialstudysf.com

TIPSY PIG
2231 Chestnut St,
San Francisco, CA 94123
thetipsypigsf.com

TOP OF THE MARK
Intercontinental Mark Hopkins,
999 California St,
San Francisco, CA 94108
intercontinentalmarkhopkins.com/
top-of-the-mark

TOYOSE
3814 Noriega St,
San Francisco, CA 94122

TRICK DOG
3010 20th St,
San Francisco, CA 94110
trickdogbar.com

TROU NORMAND
140 New Montgomery St,
San Francisco, CA 94105
trounormandsf.com

TROUBLE COFFEE
4033 Judah St,
San Francisco, CA 94122
troublecoffeeco.com

TWO SISTERS BAR AND BOOKS
579 Hayes St,
San Francisco, CA 94102
2sistersbarandbooks.com

UNA PIZZA NAPOLETANA
210 11th St,
San Francisco, CA 94103
unapizza.com

UNION SQUARE
333 Post St,
San Francisco, CA 94108
visitunionsquaresf.com

VESUVIO
255 Columbus Ave,
San Francisco, CA 94133
vesuvio.com

VISTA POINT
Golden Gate National
Recreation Area, US-101,
Sausalito, CA 94965

WAR MEMORIAL OPERA HOUSE
301 Van Ness Ave,
San Francisco, CA 94109
sfwmpac.org

WASHINGTON SQUARE PARK
Filbert and Stockton Sts,
San Francisco, CA 94133
sfrecpark.org/destination/
washington-square

WASTELAND
1660 Haight St,
San Francisco, CA 94117
shopwasteland.com

WAVE ORGAN
83 Marina Green Dr,
San Francisco, CA 94123
exploratorium.edu/visit/wave-organ

WELCOME STRANGER
460 Gough St,
San Francisco, CA 94102
welcomestranger.com

ZEITGEIST
199 Valencia St,
San Francisco, CA 94103
zeitgeistsf.com

BIKE SHOPS, CLUBS, RACES AND VENUES

ALPINE DAM LOOP
strava.com/local/us/san-francisco/
cycling/routes/601

BAY AREA BIKE SHARE
bayareabikeshare

BESPOKE CYCLES
2843 Clay St,
San Francisco, CA 94115
bespokecyclessf.com

BIKEMAPPER
sfbike.org/resources/maps-routes

BLACK SHEEP BIKE RENTAL
900 Doolittle Dr, #2b,
San Leandro, CA 94577
blacksheepbikerental.com

BLAZING SADDLES
1095 Columbus Ave,
San Francisco, CA 94133
blazingsaddles.com

CITY + COUNTY BICYCLE CO.
251 Clement St,
San Francisco, CA 94118
cityandcountybicycle.com

FREEWHEEL BIKE SHOP
1920 Hayes St,
San Francisco, CA 94117
thefreewheel.com

HAWK HILL LOOP
strava.com/local/us/san-francisco/
cycling/routes/598

HUCKLEBERRY BICYCLES
1073 Market St,
San Francisco, CA 94103
huckleberrybicycles.com

IL GIRO DE SAN FRANCISCO
bikereg.com/giro-di-san-francisco

MOJO BICYCLE CAFE
639-A Divisadero St,
San Francisco, CA 94117
mojobicyclecafe.com

PARADISE LOOP
strava.com/local/us/san-francisco/
cycling/routes/600

RAPHA CYCLE CLUB
2198 Filbert St,
San Francisco, CA 94123
pages.rapha.cc/clubs/san-francisco

SAN FRANCISCO BICYCLE COALITION
1720 Market St,
San Francisco, CA 94102
sfbike.org

SFPD ANTI BIKE THEFT
twitter.com/sfpdbiketheft

STAMMTISCH RIDE
suppenkuche.com/new/2014/03/10/
stammtisch-rides

THE WIGGLE
sfbike.org/our-work/street-
campaigns/the-wiggle

TOUR OF CALIFORNIA
amgentourofcalifornia.com

OTHER USEFUL SITES

AIRTRAN
flysfo.com/services-amenities/
getting-around-sfo

BART
bart.gov

MUNI
sfmta.com/getting-around/transit

OAKLAND INTERNATIONAL AIRPORT
1 Airport Dr,
Oakland, CA 94621
oaklandairport.com

SAN FRANCISCO INTERNATIONAL AIRPORT
San Francisco, CA 94128
flysfo.com

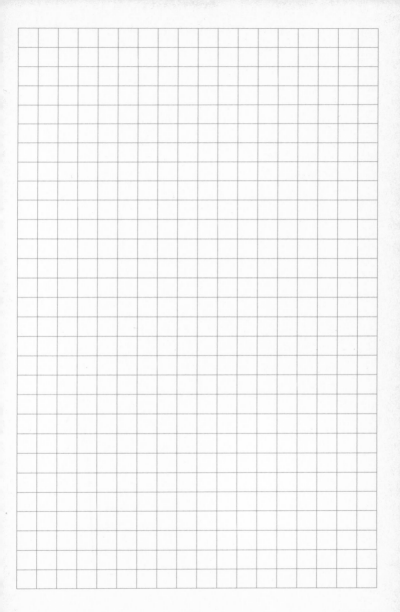

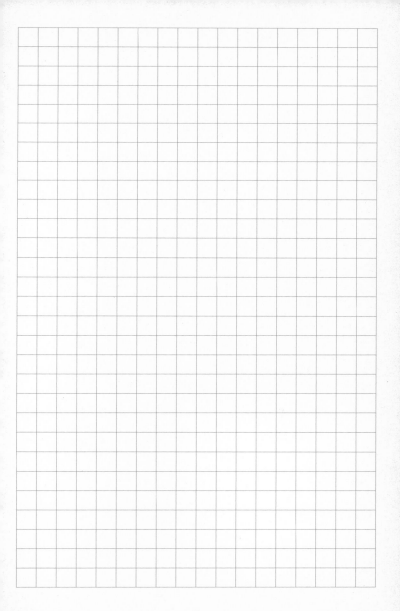

Rapha, established in London, has always been a champion of city cycling – from testing our first prototype jackets on the backs of bike couriers, to a whole range of products designed specifically for the demands of daily life on the bike. As well as an online emporium of products, films, photography and stories, Rapha has a growing network of Clubhouses, locations around the globe where cyclists can enjoy live racing, food, drink and the latest products.

Rapha.